W9-CGZ-770

CANADA: PROVINCES AND TERRITORIES

EXPLORING CANADA

Lynda Sorensen

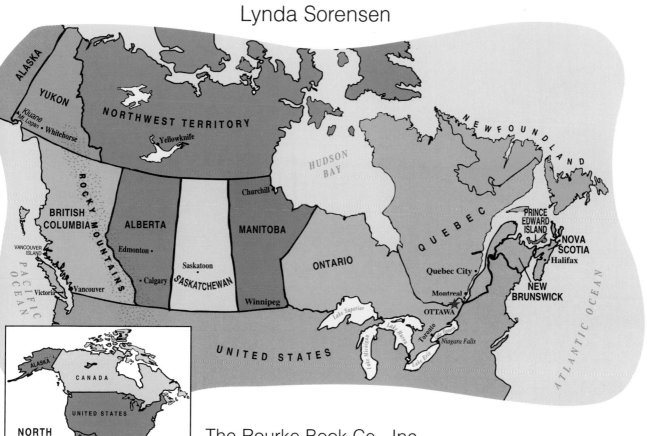

The Rourke Book Co., Inc.
Vero Beach, Florida 32964

Edited by Sandra A. Robinson and
Pamela J.P. Schroeder

PHOTO CREDITS
© Thomas Kitchin: cover, pages 4, 8, 10, 12, 13, 15; © Lynn M.
Stone: pages 7, 17, 18; © Jerry Hennen: page 21

Library of Congress Cataloging-in-Publication Data

Sorensen, Lynda, 1953-
    Canada. provinces and territories / by Lynda Sorensen.
    p. cm. — (Exploring Canada)
    Includes index.
    ISBN 1-55916-105-1
    1. Canada—Juvenile literature. 2. Canada—Administrative and
political divisions—Juvenile literature. 3. Canada—Territories and
possessions—Juvenile literature. I. Title. II. Series.
F1008.2.S67   1995
917.1—dc20   94-48248
                                                      CIP
                                                       AC

Printed in the USA

TABLE OF CONTENTS

PROVINCES AND TERRITORIES

Canada is a nation of 10 united **provinces** and two **territories.**

Like America's states, each of Canada's provinces and territories has its own government. Also like America's states, each of the provinces and territories is under a single, nationwide government. Canada's **national** government is in its capital—Ottawa, Ontario.

Canada's national government tries to help meet the needs of each province and territory. The provinces can make more of their own rules than the territories.

Queen's Park, Toronto, is the home of the Ontario Provincial Government

ATLANTIC PROVINCES

Canada is more than 3,000 miles (4,838 kilometers) wide, and reaches from the Pacific Ocean to the Atlantic Ocean. Newfoundland, New Brunswick, Prince Edward Island and Nova Scotia are the Atlantic provinces. Each province has a long Atlantic seashore.

The Atlantic provinces are famous for their fishing business. The Grand Banks, offshore from Newfoundland, has been one of the world's finest fishing grounds. However, now the fisheries are in danger from pollution in the water.

After being a separate country, Newfoundland joined Canada in 1949. It's the only country in the world to vote itself out of being a country.

Rocks hug the shore of New Brunswick, one of Canada's Atlantic provinces

QUEBEC

Quebec—Canada's largest province—is the center of French culture, or way of life.

Most people living in Quebec are French Canadians. Many of them would like Quebec to separate from the rest of Canada. They want to protect their way of life and the French language by becoming a new country.

Montreal, the largest city in Quebec, is the second-largest French-speaking city in the world after Paris, France.

Quebec has many charming villages as well as huge wilderness areas.

Percé Rock (left) lies off the town of Percé on Quebec's Gaspé Peninsula

ONTARIO

Almost one of every three Canadians lives in Ontario. Canada's largest group of **Native** people live in Ontario.

Toronto is the largest Ontario city and is close to the U.S. border.

Southern Ontario is an important business center. Many factories, banks and other businesses are there.

Northern Ontario is a wilderness of lakes, bogs and forests. Hunting and fishing attract many tourists, or visitors.

Toronto's skyline rises above the shore of Lake Ontario

Fishing is a major industry along Canada's coasts

Farm buildings nestle in the hills of Prince Edward Island, Canada's smallest province

PRAIRIE PROVINCES

Alberta, Saskatchewan and Manitoba are Canada's prairie provinces.

Much of the southern part of these provinces was prairie, or natural grassland. Now, most of the prairie has been plowed and changed into huge crop farms. This area also produces most of Canada's beef cattle, petroleum and natural gas.

The northern parts of these provinces are wilderness areas of mountains, forest and **tundra.**

Calgary, Edmonton, Winnipeg and Saskatoon are the largest cities in the prairie provinces.

Much of Alberta's old prairie now grows wheat

BRITISH COLUMBIA

British Columbia (B.C.) is Canada's seaside province in the West. Vancouver, on Canada's mainland, and Victoria, on Vancouver Island, are the major cities. Much of northern British Columbia is mountain wilderness.

Fishing, logging and **tourism** are important businesses in British Columbia.

British Columbia shares a long border—and other things—with Alaska. Students from Hyder, Alaska, on the B.C. border attend B.C. schools. People in Hyder pump gasoline in Canadian liters, instead of gallons. They freely use Canadian money—except in the post office.

British Columbia's forests supply logs and wood for countries all over the world

THE TERRITORIES

The wild, rugged country of the Yukon and Northwest Territories make up one-third of Canada's land. However, fewer than 250,000 Canadians live in this northern part of the country.

In 1999, much of the Northwest Territories will become Nunavut. The **Inuit** people will own and govern Nunavut—a new territory.

Yellowknife, the major city in the Northwest Territories, and Whitehorse, the largest city in the Yukon, will not be part of Nunavut.

Part of an old building lies in ruin in Silver City, a ghost town in the Yukon Territory

GOVERNMENT

The Canadian government, like the American government, is chosen by the people. Canadians elect the people who run the governments of the provinces and territories—and the country.

Canada's government works like England's. It is called a Parliamentary System. The **Parliament** is like America's Congress. The leader of Canada's government is called the prime minister.

Canada's national government meets in the Parliament Building in Ottawa, Ontario

HISTORY

Canada was ruled by England between 1763 and 1867.

New Brunswick, Nova Scotia, Ontario and Quebec joined together in 1867—with England's okay—to form the Dominion of Canada. The end of English rule was the first step toward forming modern-day Canada.

The Dominion of Canada added the Northwest Territories, including the Yukon, and five more provinces between 1870 and 1905.

Canada became completely free of England in 1931. Newfoundland joined Canada in 1949.

Glossary

Inuit (IN u it) — a native people of northern Canada and Alaska, often called "Eskimos" by other people

national (NA shun ul) — referring to a nation as a whole; belonging to a nation

Native (NAY tihv) — the original, or first, people who lived in Canada

Parliament (PAR luh ment) — Canada's national government

province (PRAH vints) — any one of the 10 statelike regions, which together with two territories, make up Canada

territory (TAYR uh tor ee) — either of Canada's two northern regions, which together with 10 provinces, make up Canada

tourism (TOOR iz um) — the business of attracting visitors to a place to see and learn about it

tundra (TUN druh) — the treeless carpet of low-lying plants in the Far North and on mountains above the tree line

INDEX

Park Place Elementary Library

DATE DUE			